Paddington on Stage

PLAYS FOR CHILDREN

Paddington on Stage

MICHAEL BOND
and ALFRED BRADLEY
with drawings by Peggy Fortnum

A YEARLING BOOK

Published by
Dell Publishing
a division of
Bantam Doubleday Dell Publishing Group, Inc.
666 Fifth Avenue
New York, New York 10103

Paddington on Stage is based on the play *The Adventures of Paddington Bear,* which is in turn based on the original stories by Michael Bond. The full Acting Edition of this play is published by Samuel French Ltd.

Copyright © 1974 by Alfred Bradley and Michael Bond

ISBN: 0-440-46846-9

Reprinted by arrangement with Houghton Mifflin Company

Printed in the United States of America

One Previous Edition

March 1992

10 9 8 7 6 5 4 3 2 1

OPM

Contents

Introduction   7

Costume Notes   9

1. The Arrival of Paddington   13

2. Paddington Paints a Picture   31

3. Paddington Has a Birthday   45

4. Paddington Visits the Dentist   57

5. Paddington Goes to the Launderette   67

6. Paddington Goes to the Hospital   77

7. Paddington Turns Detective   93

Songs   109

Over the years lots of children have written in asking "Why isn't there a Paddington play?", and as many again have told of their efforts in schools, or at home in the spare room, the garage, or outside in the garden, to put on a play of their own.

Towards the end of 1973 the first group were catered for when *The Adventures of a Bear Called Paddington* opened at the Nottingham Playhouse.

Paddington On Stage is meant for those who like to "do-it-themselves". It's really a selection of playlets from the professional version with all the complicated trimmings – the sets, the props, and some of the more difficult dialogue taken out. You can add to it, take away from it, even make up your own words as you go along; no-one, least of all Paddington, will mind in the slightest.

In short, it's for all children who like to dress-up, play make-believe, or simply have fun – with or without an audience, and to whom a board with two words painted on it turns a room into Paddington Station, and someone wearing an old hat and some wellington boots (plus maybe a duffle-coat if there's one around) becomes Paddington himself.

Michael Bond.

Costume Notes

If you already know the Paddington books, or have read these plays, then you will probably have a picture in your mind's eye of what the main characters look like and how to act them.

It's really very simple: MR and MRS BROWN are the kind of people who *would* take a bear home to live with them. That is to say, they are warm-hearted and rather vague.

MR BROWN is a little less happy about the whole thing than his wife, but only because he feels there may be a law against it. He works in a city office, and this can be suggested by having him carry a rolled umbrella and a folded newspaper when he leaves home; also a briefcase if one is available. He would also wear a hat – a bowler is ideal – but a dark trilby is almost as good. He can have a moustache and glasses – lots of toy or joke shops stock this kind of thing, but a pair of old, unwanted sunglasses with the plastic lenses taken out would be fine. His chin can be darkened slightly with the aid of burnt cork, and age can be suggested by drawing in the "crow's feet" around the eyes with an eyebrow pencil or a black felt pen. The easiest way to find these lines is to stand in front of a mirror, screw up your eyes, then relax them again. But always remember it is better to have too little make-up than too much.

MRS BROWN is well-dressed without being too smart. If you are able to borrow a wig or hair-piece it will help, but even combing your own hair a different way can make a lot of difference to your appearance. She should wear a little make-up, some lipstick and rouge, but again not too much.

The Browns have two children, JONATHAN and JUDY. They are both at school, and secretly rather proud of having a bear about the house. They are also slightly envious of Paddington's ability to get into a mess and still come out on top. As a contrast to the other characters they can wear school clothes.

MRS BIRD, the housekeeper, is older than the Browns and on the surface much more stern. But deep down she is just as soft-hearted and would protect Paddington through thick and thin. She would normally wear her hair in a bun, and it can be made grey, or even white, by combing in some talcum powder. Very pale make-up on the lips is another way of suggesting age. An effective white wig can be made by gluing cotton wool to an old shower cap. She would wear a fairly long skirt, and perhaps a shawl.

Paddington's friend, MR GRUBER, who keeps an antique shop in the Portobello Road, is himself an immigrant from Central Europe, so he has a special relationship with Paddington and understands how it feels to live in a country which isn't really your own. They have a great respect for each other and always use their surnames. He also wears glasses, but steel-rimmed if possible, perched on the end of his nose so that he can look over the top. He walks with a slight stoop and speaks with a hint of a foreign accent. His clothes can be well-worn, comfortable without being down-at-heel.

Last, but not least, is MR CURRY, the Browns' neighbour. He has a reputation for being bad-tempered, with a way of barking out commands rather than holding a conversation. He doesn't approve of Paddington's "goings-on" and never loses an opportunity of telling him so. He should be played "tight-lipped", and with a habit of drawing in his breath as if he is about to explode at any moment.

As suggested in the foreword, PADDINGTON himself can be played by someone dressed in a duffle-coat, wellington boots, and a battered old 1920's style hat. If you have a willing parent, who is also handy with a needle and thread, it might even be possible to make a costume out of some suitable material, but as Paddington is the sort of bear who happily wears his duffle-coat at all times, this is not as important as it might be. (He doesn't actually have it when he is found on Paddington Station, but for the plays this point could be overlooked – it's what is known as "dramatic licence!") He has a strong sense of right and wrong, and a "hard stare" which he often uses when he is upset by something. This could be "pointed" by someone behind the scenes "pinging" a ruler on the edge of a desk. His voice is best played as you hear it in your own head; perhaps a rather high-pitched but gruff voice, if such a thing exists!

There is no need to have a stage as such, or even curtains – lots of theatres nowadays have gone back to the open stage, but if the acting area can have more light than the part where the audience are sitting, then so much the better. At the back of the book you will find the words of two songs from the original stage production. The first *I Try So Hard* can be sung by Paddington himself as an alternative ending for any of the plays other than the first one where it's best if he simply falls asleep. The second song *Paddington Bear* can be used to round off the final play instead of *For He's a Jolly Good Bear Cub*. It will also add a professional touch to have some suitable music on a record player at the beginning and end, and during scene changes or intervals. If the scene changes are done in front of the audience, then fun can be had by doing it in time to the music and turning it into a part of the production. The actors themselves can help out, and if it's well done you may even get a round of applause for that too!

The Arrival of Paddington

CAST OF CHARACTERS

MR BROWN
MRS BROWN
PADDINGTON BEAR
REFRESHMENT MAN
JUDY BROWN
MRS BIRD
JONATHAN BROWN

PROPS

At Paddington Station:
Cardboard boxes
Sign saying "Paddington Station"
Suitcase
Jar of marmalade – almost empty
Tea trolley or tray
*Cakes on paper plates
Plastic or paper cups
Drinking straw
*Cake wrapper

At Number thirty-two, Windsor Gardens:
Table and chairs
Tray with teapot and cups
Towel
Possibly some cushions and anything
else that helps make the set look like
the Browns' living room.

The play starts on Paddington Station. All that we need is a heap of parcels to hide PADDINGTON, (cardboard boxes will do) and a sign saying "Paddington Station". PADDINGTON wears a floppy bush hat, wellington boots and has a label tied round his neck which says "Please look after this bear. Thank you." In his suitcase, which he takes with him wherever he goes, is a jar of marmalade. When the refreshment man arrives he should have a tea trolley or a tray with several plastic or paper cups and some sticky cakes. *(As real cakes may be messy, it is probably best to make your own using Krazy Foam or shaving cream which will wash off easily.) *The sticky cake wrapper can be made out of an ordinary cake wrapper, covered on both sides with double-sided, transparent sticky tape.

When we get to Number thirty-two, Windsor Gardens we will need a table, and some chairs. You can make the splashing and banging for Paddington's shower by hammering on something noisy (an old biscuit tin would do) and by splashing water in a bucket.

Scene One

When the play begins PADDINGTON is concealed behind an assorted pile of parcels and luggage. HENRY BROWN comes on to the platform, closely followed by his wife.

MR BROWN   Well, Mary, after all that rushing about, we're here early.

MRS BROWN   What's the time now?

MR BROWN   It's just a quarter past four and Judy's train doesn't arrive until half past.

MRS BROWN   Are you sure?

MR BROWN   She told me in her letter and she doesn't usually make mistakes.

MRS BROWN   I'll just go and check which platform . . . [goes off]

[Left to himself MR BROWN strolls around the platform. PADDINGTON, hidden behind the parcels, pops up like a jack-in-the-box and quickly down again. MR BROWN is looking surprised; MRS BROWN returns]

MRS BROWN   It's platform five. And you're quite right, the train doesn't arrive until half past four.

MR BROWN   Mary, you won't believe this, but I've just seen a bear.

MRS BROWN   A what?

MR BROWN   A bear.

MRS BROWN   A bear? On Paddington Station. Don't be silly, Henry. There can't be.

MR BROWN   But there is. I distinctly saw it. Over there. Behind those parcels. It was wearing a funny kind of hat. Come and see for yourself.

MRS BROWN   [*humouring him*] Very well. [*She peers behind the parcels*] Why Henry, I believe you were right after all. It is a bear!

[PADDINGTON *stands up suddenly. He is wearing a bush hat with a wide brim and has a large luggage label round his neck*]

PADDINGTON   Good afternoon. [*He raises his hat*]

MR BROWN   Er . . . good afternoon.

PADDINGTON   Can I help you?

MR BROWN   Well . . . no. Er, not really. As a matter of fact, we were wondering if we could help you.

MRS BROWN   [*taking a closer look*] You're a very unusual bear.

PADDINGTON   I'm a very rare sort of bear. There aren't many of us left where I come from.

MR BROWN   And where is that?

PADDINGTON   Darkest Peru. I'm not really supposed to be here at all. I'm a stowaway.

MRS BROWN   A stowaway?

PADDINGTON   Yes. I emigrated you know. I used to live with my Aunt Lucy in Peru, but she had to go into a Home for Retired Bears.

MRS BROWN   You don't mean to say you've come all the way from South America by yourself?

PADDINGTON   Yes. Aunt Lucy always said she wanted me to emigrate when I was old enough. That's why she taught me to speak English.

MR BROWN   But whatever did you do for food? You must be starving.

PADDINGTON [*opening his suitcase and taking out an almost empty jar*] I ate marmalade. Bears like marmalade. And I hid in a lifeboat.

MR BROWN But what are you going to do now? You can't just sit on Paddington Station waiting for something to happen.

PADDINGTON Oh, I shall be all right . . . I expect.

MRS BROWN What does it say on your label?

MR BROWN [*reading it*] "Please look after this bear. Thank you."

MRS BROWN That must be from his Aunt Lucy. Oh, Henry, what shall we do? We can't just leave him here. There's no knowing what might happen to him. Can't he come and stay with us for a few days?

MR BROWN But Mary, dear, we can't take him . . . not just like that. After all . . .

MRS BROWN After all, what? He'd be good company for Jonathan and Judy. Even if it's only for a little while. They'd never forgive us if they knew you'd left him here.

MR BROWN It all seems highly irregular. I'm sure there's a law against it. [*Turning to* PADDINGTON] Would you like to come and stay with us? That is, if you've nothing else planned.

PADDINGTON [*overjoyed*] Oooh, yes, please. I should like that very much. I've nowhere to go and everyone seems in such a hurry.

MRS BROWN Well, that's settled then. And you can have marmalade for breakfast every morning . . .

PADDINGTON Every morning? I only had it on special occasions at home. Marmalade's very expensive in Darkest Peru.

MRS BROWN Then you shall have it every morning starting tomorrow.

PADDINGTON [*worried*] Will it cost a lot? You see I haven't very much money.

MRS BROWN Of course not. We wouldn't dream of charging you anything. We shall expect you to be one of the family, shan't we Henry.

MR BROWN Of course. By the way, if you *are* coming home with us you'd better know our names. This is Mrs Brown and I'm Mr Brown.

PADDINGTON [*raises his hat twice*] I haven't really got a name, only a Peruvian one which no one can understand.

MRS BROWN Then we'd better give you an English one. It'll make things much easier. [*Thinking hard*] It ought to be something special. Now what shall we call you? I know! We found you on Paddington Station so that's what we'll call you . . . Paddington.

PADDINGTON [*savouring it*] Paddington. Pad-ding-ton. Paddington. It seems a very long name.

MR BROWN It's quite distinguished. Yes, I like Paddington as a name. Paddington it shall be.

MRS BROWN Good. Now, Paddington, I have to meet our young daughter Judy off the train. I'm sure you must be thirsty after your long journey, so while I'm away Mr Brown will get you something to drink.

PADDINGTON Thank you.

MRS BROWN And for goodness sake, Henry, when you get a moment, take that label off his neck. It makes him look like a parcel.

[PADDINGTON *doesn't much like the thought of looking like a parcel*]

I'm sure he'll get put in a luggage van if a porter sees him. [*She goes off almost bumping into a* MAN *pushing the refreshment trolley*]

MR BROWN [*removing the label*] There we are. Ah! The very thing. Now I can get you something to drink.

[PADDINGTON *puts the luggage label into his suitcase*]

MAN What would you like, tea or coffee?

PADDINGTON Cocoa, please.

MAN [*annoyed*] We haven't got any cocoa.

PADDINGTON But you asked me what I would like . . .

MAN I asked you what would you like, *tea* or *coffee*!

MR BROWN [*hastily, trying to avoid an argument*] Perhaps you'd like a cold drink?

MAN Lemonade or orangeade?

PADDINGTON Marmalade.

MR BROWN [*before the man loses his temper*] I think some orangeade would be a good idea – and a cup of tea for me, please.

[*The* MAN *serves them*]

And perhaps you'd like a cake, Paddington?

PADDINGTON Oooh, yes, please.

MAN   Cream-and-chocolate, or cream-and-jam?

PADDINGTON Yes, please.

MAN   Well, which do you want?

MR BROWN We'd better have one of each.

[*The* MAN *puts them on a plate.* MR BROWN *pays him, and hands the plate to* PADDINGTON]

             How's that to be going on with?

PADDINGTON It's very nice, thank you, Mr Brown. But it's not very easy drinking out of a beaker. I usually get my nose stuck.

MR BROWN Perhaps you'd like a straw. [*He takes one from the* MAN *and puts it into Paddington's beaker*]

PADDINGTON That's a good idea. [*He blows through the straw and makes a noisy bubbling sound*] I'm glad I emigrated. [*Takes a bite from one of the cakes*] I wonder what else there is?

[*He puts the plate of cakes on the floor in order to peer at the trolley and promptly steps on the cake. In his excitement he upsets the rest of the cups on the trolley, scattering them in all directions. Trying to steady himself, he knocks Mr Brown's tea out of his hand, slips over and ends up sprawled on the platform. As* MR BROWN *bends to help him up* PADDINGTON *staggers to his feet. They collide and* PADDINGTON's *cream cake ends up plastered all over* MR BROWN's *face. Just at this moment* MRS BROWN *returns with* JUDY. *All this will need to be carefully rehearsed beforehand*]

MRS BROWN Henry! Henry, whatever are you doing to that poor bear? Look at him! He's covered all over with jam and cream.

MR BROWN   *He's* covered with jam and cream! What about me? [*He begins to tidy up the mess*]

MRS BROWN   This is what happens when I leave your father alone for five minutes.

JUDY   [*clapping her hands*] Oh, Daddy, is he really going to stay with us?

[PADDINGTON *stands up, raises his hat, steps on the cake and falls over again*]

Oh, Mummy, isn't he funny!

MRS BROWN   You wouldn't think that anybody could get in such a state with just one cake.

MR BROWN   Perhaps we'd better go. Are we all ready?

JUDY   Come along, Paddington.

[PADDINGTON *picks up his suitcase and puts the remains of the cakes in it. The cake wrapper sticks to his paws but he doesn't notice it*]

We'll go straight home and you can have a nice hot bath. Then you can tell me all about South America. I'm sure you must have had lots of wonderful adventures.

PADDINGTON   I have. Lots. Things are always happening to me, I'm that sort of bear. [*He goes off with* JUDY]

MR BROWN   [*to his wife*] I hope we haven't bitten off more than we can chew.

MAN   Well, if you have, you'll just have to grin and *bear* it. [*He laughs loudly at his own joke and goes off*]

Scene Two

[*Number thirty-two, Windsor Gardens.* JUDY *and* PAD-DINGTON *have just walked into the living room*]

JUDY   Here we are. Now you are going to meet Mrs Bird.

PADDINGTON   Mrs Bird?

JUDY   Yes. She looks after us. She's a bit fierce sometimes and she grumbles a bit, but she doesn't really mean it. I'm sure you'll like her.

PADDINGTON   [*nervously*] I'm sure I shall, if you say so.

[*The door opens and* MRS BIRD *appears*]

MRS BIRD   Goodness gracious, you've arrived already, and me hardly finished the washing up. I suppose you'll be wanting tea?

JUDY   Hello, Mrs Bird. It's nice to see you again. How's the rheumatism?

MRS BIRD   Worse than it's ever been. [*She stops abruptly as she sees* PADDINGTON] Good gracious! Whatever have you got there?

JUDY   It's not a what, Mrs Bird. It's a bear. His name's Paddington.

[PADDINGTON *raises his hat*]

MRS BIRD   A bear . . . well, he has good manners, I'll say that for him.

JUDY   He's going to stay with us. He's come all the way from South America and he's all alone with nowhere to go.

MRS BIRD   Going to *stay* with us? How long for?

JUDY   I don't know. I suppose it *depends*!

MRS BIRD   Mercy me. I wish you'd told me he was
                coming. I haven't put clean sheets in the
                spare room or anything.

PADDINGTON   It's all right, Mrs Bird. I didn't have any
                sheets in the lifeboat. I'm sure I shall be very
                comfortable.

[*He shakes hands with her. When he lets go, the leftover
cake wrapper is sticking to her hand. She tries in vain to get
it off, and finally it sticks to her other hand*]

JUDY   Let me help, Mrs Bird. [JUDY *takes it from
                her, but then finds that it is glued to her own
                hand*]

[*At this moment* MR *and* MRS BROWN *arrive with*
JONATHAN]

                Hello, Jonathan. [*She shakes hands with*
                JONATHAN *and passes the sticky paper on to
                him*] You haven't met Paddington yet, have
                you? Paddington, this is my brother
                Jonathan.

JONATHAN   How do you do?

PADDINGTON   Very well, thank you.

[PADDINGTON *shakes hands with* JONATHAN *and
collects the sticky paper*]

MRS BIRD   Whatever's going on?

PADDINGTON   I'm afraid I had an accident with a cake,
                Mrs Bird. It's left me a bit sticky.

MRS BIRD   I think a good hot bath will do you the
                world of good.

JUDY   [*confidentially*] She doesn't mind really. In
                fact, I think she rather likes you.

PADDINGTON   She seems a bit fierce.

MRS BIRD   [*turning round suddenly*] What was that?

PADDINGTON   I didn't hear anything.

MRS BIRD   Where was it you said you'd come from?
                Peru?

PADDINGTON   That's right. *Darkest* Peru.

MRS BIRD   Humph. Then I expect you like marma-
                lade. I'd better get some more from the
                grocer. [*She leaves the room*]

JUDY   [*happily*] There you are! What did I tell
                you? She *does* like you.

PADDINGTON   Fancy her knowing that I like marmalade.

JUDY   Mrs Bird knows everything about every-
                thing.

MRS BROWN   Now, Judy, you'd better show Paddington
                his room.

JUDY   Come on. It used to be mine when I was
                small. There's a bathroom as well so you
                can have a good clean up.

PADDINGTON   A *bathroom*. Fancy having a special room for
                a bath.

        [*They leave the room*]

MR BROWN   I hope we're doing the right thing.

MRS BROWN   Well, we can hardly turn him out now. It
                wouldn't be fair.

MR BROWN   I'm sure we ought to report the matter to someone first.

JONATHAN   I don't see why, Dad. Besides, didn't you say he was a stowaway? He might get arrested.

MR BROWN   Then there's the question of pocket money. I'm not sure how much money to give a bear.

MRS BROWN   He can have twenty pence a week, the same as Jonathan and Judy.

MR BROWN   Very well, but we'll have to see what Mrs Bird has to say about it first.

JONATHAN   Hurrah!

MRS BROWN   *You'd* better ask her then, it was your idea.

[MRS BIRD *comes in with a tray of tea, followed by* JUDY]

MRS BIRD   I suppose you want to tell me you've decided to keep that young Paddington.

JUDY   May we, Mrs Bird? *Please.* I'm sure he'll be very good.

MRS BIRD   Humph! [*She puts the tray on the table*] That remains to be seen. Different people have different ideas about being good. All the same, he looks the sort of bear who means well.

MR BROWN   Then you don't mind, Mrs Bird?

MRS BIRD   No. No, I don't mind at all. I've always had a soft spot for bears myself. It'll be nice to have one about the house. [*She goes*]

MR BROWN   Well, whoever would have thought it?

JUDY   I expect it was because he raised his hat. It
                   made a good impression.

MRS BROWN   [pouring the tea] I suppose someone ought to
                   write and tell his Aunt Lucy. I'm sure she'd
                   like to know how he's getting on.

MR BROWN   By the way, how *is* he getting on?

[*There is a loud gurgling noise from the bath, followed by a
tremendous splashing sound.* PADDINGTON *begins to
sing*]

JUDY   Oh, all right, I think. At least, he seemed all
                   right when I left him.

[MR BROWN *suddenly feels his head*]

MR BROWN   That's funny. I could have sworn I felt a
                   spot of water.

MRS BROWN   Don't be silly, Henry. How could you?

MR BROWN   [another drop lands on his head] It's happened
                   again!

JONATHAN   [looks up at the ceiling] Crikey! [He nudges
                   JUDY] Look!

JUDY   [looks up too] Oh, gosh! The bath!

JONATHAN   Come on!

MR BROWN   Where are you two going?

JUDY   Oh . . . [pretending to be casual] We're just
                   going upstairs to see how Paddington's
                   getting on. [She bundles JONATHAN out of
                   the room] Quick!

MRS BROWN   What was all that about, I wonder?

MR BROWN   I don't know, Mary. I suppose they're just
                   excited about having a bear in the house . . .

JUDY   [calls offstage] Are you all right, Paddington?

PADDINGTON   Yes, I think so.

JUDY   Gosh! Look at the mess.

JONATHAN   Why on earth didn't you turn the tap off?
                No wonder all the water overflowed.

PADDINGTON   I'm afraid I got soap in my eyes. I couldn't
                see anything.

[As he is led back into the room by JONATHAN and
JUDY, he squeezes water out of his hat]

                It's a good thing I had my hat with me. I
                used it to bail the water out. I might have
                drowned otherwise.

MR BROWN   No wonder I thought I felt some water.

JUDY   Now you just dry yourself properly, or
                you'll catch cold. [She drapes a towel round
                him]

PADDINGTON   [proudly as he looks at himself] I'm a lot
                cleaner than I was.

[MRS BIRD enters]

MRS BIRD   You'd better give me your hat, Paddington.
                I'll put it on the line.

PADDINGTON   [puts his hat back on] I'd rather you didn't,
                Mrs Bird. I don't like being without it. It's
                my special bush hat and it belonged to my
                uncle.

MRS BROWN   In that case, perhaps you'd like to tell us all
                about yourself, and how you came to
                emigrate.

PADDINGTON   [sits down in an armchair and makes the most of

his audience] Well . . . I was brought up by
my Aunt Lucy. [*He closes his eyes*]

JONATHAN   Your Aunt Lucy?

PADDINGTON [*sleepily*] Yes. She's the one who lives in the
Home for Retired Bears in [SNORE]-ima . . .

MR BROWN   [*puzzled*] In [SNORE]-ima! Where's that?

PADDINGTON It's in Peru, Mr Brown. [SNORE] *Darkest*
Peru.

JUDY   Paddington . . . wake up.

[PADDINGTON *gives a longer snore.* MR BROWN *pokes
him gently*]

MR BROWN   Well I never. I do believe he's fallen asleep.

MRS BROWN   [*drapes the towel round him to make him more
comfortable*] I'm not really surprised. I don't
suppose there are many bears who've had
quite such a busy day!

JONATHAN
JUDY   [*in chorus*] Especially from [SNORE]-ima.

CURTAIN

Paddington Paints a Picture

CAST OF CHARACTERS

MR BROWN

PADDINGTON

MR GRUBER

MRS BIRD

MISS BLACK

JONATHAN

JUDY

MAN

PROPS

In the Browns' sitting room:
A few chairs
Table
Easel

(for scenes III and IV):
Very messy painting
Paint brush
Paints – red and green
Marmalade jar
Spoon
Palette (can be made from cardboard)
Three empty bottles, painted to look as
if they contain paint remover, ketchup
and mustard
Handkerchief
Washing-up liquid
Slip of paper for cheque

In Mr Gruber's shop:
Chair
Sign saying "Antiques"
Thermos flask, two mugs and a bun
Pile of bric-a-brac, china, books, toys
*Half-restored "painting"

In this play the easel with Mr Brown's painting should be placed near the centre of the stage so that Paddington has plenty of room to work on it. We don't need to see the painting, as it will be facing away from us until Miss Black brings it back at the end of the play. Of course, the tomato ketchup and mustard and paint remover should not be real (use empty bottles painted to look full), and the painting should be done beforehand so that it is dry for the performance. The painting should look as messy as you can make it.

When we get to Mr Gruber's shop, all that we need to see is a pile of oddments with a notice saying "Antiques". Mr Gruber should have a chair to sit on, *a half-cleaned picture with a boat on one side and part of a lady's face on the other, a thermos flask and two mugs.

Scene One

[*The Browns' sitting room.* MR BROWN *is getting ready to go to work as* PADDINGTON *comes in. The easel is standing with its back to the audience*]

MR BROWN   Hello, Paddington, what are your plans for today?

PADDINGTON   I think I might do some shopping, Mr Brown. I like shopping.

MR BROWN   You won't get lost?

PADDINGTON   No, I won't be going very far. Is your painting finished, Mr Brown?

MR BROWN   Yes. [*He looks at it*] You know, I really think it's the best I've ever done.

PADDINGTON   I hope you win a prize.

MR BROWN   Oh, I don't expect I shall. But it's fun, that's the important thing, I suppose. I must be off now, I'm late for work already. [*He goes to the door*] Goodbye, Paddington. I'll see you tonight.

PADDINGTON   Goodbye, Mr Brown.

[MR BROWN *goes, and* PADDINGTON *takes a closer look at the painting*]

I think I would enjoy painting. It looks *very* interesting.

Scene Two

[*Mr Gruber's bric-a-brac shop in the Portobello Road. He is cleaning an oil painting when* PADDINGTON *arrives*]

MR GRUBER   Good morning. Can I help you?

34

PADDINGTON [*putting down his suitcase*] I don't know really. I was out for a walk and your shop looked so nice, I thought I would like to see inside.

MR GRUBER Please have a look round, Mr . . . er . . .

PADDINGTON Brown. Paddington Brown. I come from Darkest Peru.

MR GRUBER Darkest Peru? How strange. I know Peru quite well. I spent a lot of my early life in South America.

PADDINGTON Fancy that, Mr . . . er . . .

MR GRUBER Gruber. Look . . . I've just made some cocoa, Mr Brown. Would you care for a cup?

PADDINGTON Ooh, yes, please.

MR GRUBER It's quite hot. I keep it in a vacuum.

PADDINGTON [*amazed*] You keep your cocoa in a vacuum cleaner?

MR GRUBER No, Mr Brown, a vacuum flask. [*He pours some cocoa and hands it to* PADDINGTON] There's nothing like a chat over a bun and a cup of cocoa.

PADDINGTON A bun as well! [*They sit down to enjoy their elevenses*] What were you doing when I came into the shop, Mr Gruber?

MR GRUBER I was cleaning a painting. [*He picks it up*] Now, what do you think of that?

PADDINGTON [*looking at it*] It's a puzzle, Mr Gruber. One half is a boat and the other half is a lady in a large hat.

35

MR GRUBER   There you are. I'd like your opinion on it, Mr Brown.

PADDINGTON   It doesn't seem to be one thing or the other.

MR GRUBER   Ah! It isn't at the moment. But just you wait until I've cleaned it! I gave five shillings for that painting years and years ago, when it was just a picture of a sailing ship. And what do you think? When I started to clean it the other day, all the paint began to come off and I discovered that there was another painting underneath. [*Confidentially*] It could be an old master.

PADDINGTON   An old master? It looks like an old lady to me.

MR GRUBER   [*laughs*] What I mean is, it could be very valuable. It could be by a famous painter.

PADDINGTON   That sounds interesting. Very interesting indeed. [*He gets up, his mind obviously elsewhere*] I'll have to be going now, Mr Gruber. Thank you for the elevenses.

MR GRUBER   Is anything the matter, Mr Brown?

PADDINGTON   No, Mr Gruber. I've had an idea, that's all. [*Mysteriously, as he makes to leave*] I may come into some money soon.

MR GRUBER   Good day, Mr Brown. I shall look forward to that. [*He watches* PADDINGTON *go*] Come into some money! I wonder what he meant by that?

Scene Three

[*The Browns' sitting room.* PADDINGTON *comes in, looks round carefully. He takes a bottle of paint remover from his coat pocket. He soaks a handkerchief in paint remover and rubs it over the painting. He stands back to look, and horrified by what he sees, decides to have another try. He is giving the painting a vigorous scrub when* MRS BIRD *enters*]

MRS BIRD Now, Paddington, what are you up to? I thought you were out shopping.

PADDINGTON I was. But I'm not any more. [*Gloomily*] I wish I still was.

MRS BIRD Whatever's the matter? [*She sees the picture*] What *have* you been doing? That's the painting Mr Brown did specially for the exhibition.

PADDINGTON I know. I thought there might be an old master underneath.

MRS BIRD An old master? [*She looks at the painting*] It used to be some boats on a lake. It looks more like a storm at sea now. He'll be most upset when he sees it.

PADDINGTON I know, Mrs Bird, what can I do?

MRS BIRD They're coming to collect it today. There's only one hope, perhaps you could touch it up before they get here.

PADDINGTON That's a good idea, Mrs Bird. Except I haven't any paints.

MRS BIRD There's an old box under the stairs. I'll get them for you. [*She goes*]

PADDINGTON   I wonder if it will work. [*He gets a jar of marmalade, takes a spoonful, and then puts it on the table near the easel*]

MRS BIRD   [*coming in with a paintbox and palette*] Here we are. It's very old, but it's the best I can do.

PADDINGTON   Thank you, Mrs Bird.

MRS BIRD   I hope you manage something. I don't know I'm sure . . . [*She goes to the kitchen*]

PADDINGTON   [*holding the brush at arm's length, he considers the canvas*] Uh, huh. [*He squeezes a tube of red paint on the palette, then he does the same with a green tube. He begins to paint boldly. Although we can't see the painting, it is obvious that he is making a mess*] That looks better! [*Throughout this painting scene* PADDINGTON *occasionally touches the brush to his face, without realizing he is giving himself red and green spots. He dabs at the painting, absent-mindedly dipping his brush into the marmalade, and then decides to experiment. First he adds some mustard, and then the contents of a washing-up liquid squeezer and a bottle of tomato ketchup*] There's one thing about painting, it's fun. [*He makes a huge mess of it.* MISS BLACK *arrives to collect the picture and knocks at the front door.* PADDINGTON *puts down his brush and goes to the door*]

MISS BLACK   Good afternoon. I believe Mr Brown has a painting for our exhibition.

PADDINGTON   Oh, yes. That's right. I'll get it for you. [*He goes back, gives the painting a finishing dab, wipes the brush on his hat, and takes the painting to the front door*]

MISS BLACK   Thank you very much. The final judging takes place this afternoon.

PADDINGTON   The *final* judging?

MISS BLACK   Yes, we shall be awarding the prizes today. I expect you will hear the results later this evening. Goodbye. [*She goes*]

PADDINGTON   Goodbye. There's something else about painting – it's fun while it lasts, but it's much more difficult than it looks. I can't think what Mr Brown will say . . .

Scene Four

[*Later that day. The* BROWN *family are in the sitting room after dinner*]

MRS BROWN   Would you like a cup of cocoa, Paddington?

PADDINGTON   No, thank you.

MRS BROWN   Are you all right?

PADDINGTON   Yes, I thank so, think you. I mean, I think so, thank you.

MRS BROWN   Nothing on your mind?

PADDINGTON   No.

JONATHAN   How about a bull's-eye?

PADDINGTON   No, thank you. I think I'll just go and have a rest for a bit. [*He goes out of the room*]

MRS BROWN	I do hope he's all right, Henry. He hardly touched his dinner, and that's not like him at all. And he seemed to have some funny red spots all over his face.
JONATHAN	Red spots! I wonder if it's measles. I hope he's given it to me, whatever it is. Then I will be able to stay away from school.
JUDY	Well, he's got green ones as well. I distinctly saw them.
MR BROWN	Green ones! I wonder if he's sickening for something? If they're not gone in the morning, we'd better send for the doctor.
JONATHAN	They're judging the paintings today, aren't they, Dad?
MR BROWN	Yes, they took mine away this afternoon.
JONATHAN	Do you think you'll win a prize?
MRS BROWN	No one will be more surprised than your father if he does. He's never won a prize yet.
MR BROWN	It took me a long while but I don't suppose I'll be any luckier than last time. The lady who collected it this afternoon told Paddington that the results would be made known today, so we'll soon know.
JUDY	I wonder if he's feeling any better? [*She goes out*]
JONATHAN	Perhaps they have *green* measles in Darkest Peru.

[*There is a knock at the front door.* MRS BIRD *goes to answer it*]

MRS BIRD   Who can that be?

[MRS BIRD *opens the door.* MISS BLACK *is waiting out-side. She has a* MAN *with her. He is carrying Mr Brown's painting, still with its back to the audience*]

MISS BLACK   Good evening. Is Mr Brown in?

MAN   We've come about the painting he entered for our competition.

MRS BIRD   Oh, dear. Will you come this way, please?
               [*She ushers them into the room*]

MAN   Mr Brown?

MR BROWN   That's right.

MAN   I'm the President of the Art Society, and this is Miss Black, who was one of the judges of the competition.

MR BROWN   How do you do.

MAN   I've some news for you, Mr Brown.

PADDINGTON   [*offstage*] Ooooooh!

MISS BLACK   Good gracious! What was that?

MAN   It sounded like a cow mooing somewhere.

MRS BROWN   I think it's only a bear oooohing.

MAN   Oh! Er . . . Mr Brown, as I was saying, the judges decided that your painting was most unusual . . .

MRS BIRD   It certainly was.

MAN   And they have all agreed to award you the first prize.

MR BROWN   The *first* prize?

MISS BLACK   Yes, they thought your painting showed great imagination.

MR BROWN   [*pleased*] Did they now?

MAN   It made great use of marmalade chunks.

THE BROWNS   [*chorus*] Marmalade chunks!

MAN   Yes, indeed. I don't think I've ever come
              across anything quite like it before [*He
              places the painting on the easel facing the
              audience. It is, to say the least, unusual, and
              there are several real marmalade chunks sticking
              to it*]

MRS BROWN   I didn't know you were interested in
              abstract art, Henry.

MR BROWN   Nor did I!

      [PADDINGTON *and* JUDY *put their heads round the door*]

MAN   [*he removes a marmalade chunk with a flourish
              and swallows it*] It not only looks good – it
              tastes good!

MISS BLACK   What are you calling it?

MR BROWN   Where's Paddington?

MISS BLACK   Where's Paddington? What a funny title!

MAN   Well, sir, my congratulations! We'll be
              wanting the painting back in a day or so to
              put into the exhibition, but I'll leave it with
              you for the moment. Just one more thing
              . . . your prize. [*He hands over a cheque*] £10.

MISS BLACK   May I ask what you will do with it, Mr
              Brown?

MR BROWN   [*wearily*] I think perhaps I'd better give it to
              a certain Home for Retired Bears in South
              America.

MAN   Oh, really? Well, we must be getting along.
            [*As they leave* PADDINGTON *falls into the room.* JUDY
            follows him in]

MRS BIRD   Well, Paddington. The secret's out. Now,
            what have you got to say for yourself?

PADDINGTON [*crosses to the painting. He removes a marma-*
            lade chunk and goes to eat it] I think it looks
            good enough to eat, Mr Brown! [*He*
            turns it up the other way] But I think they
            might have put it the right way up. After
            all, it's not every day a bear wins first prize
            in a painting competition.

CURTAIN

Paddington Has a Birthday

CAST OF CHARACTERS

MR GRUBER
PADDINGTON
MRS BROWN
MRS BIRD
JUDY
JONATHAN
MR CURRY
MR BROWN

PROPS

In Mr Gruber's shop:
Piles of bric-a-brac
Two chairs
Candlestick
Two mugs
Cardboard box (the conjuring set) and "magic wand"
Small table
Paddington's suitcase and marmalade jar
*Long cloth
Small cloth
Book

In the Browns' sitting room
Chairs and table
Cake (not necessarily a real cake)
Candle
Matches
Plates
*Egg
Small packet (Paddington's sandwich)
*Toy watch
Toy rubber hammer

Mr Gruber's shop is just as we saw it in the last play. The conjuring set is simple to make: you will need a short rod to use as a wand and a small table covered by a *long cloth, with a pocket hanging down at the back. PADDINGTON will need to practise making the egg disappear and producing the marmalade with the help of the pocket.

*For the egg, use a broken eggshell that has been glued or sellotaped together.

*Mr Curry's watch can be made using a wide rubber band for the strap and a milkbottle top for the face.

Scene One

[*Mr Gruber's shop in the Portobello Road.* MR GRUBER *is polishing an old candlestick when* PADDINGTON *arrives. He is carrying his suitcase containing a jar of marmalade*]

MR GRUBER   Good morning, Mr Brown.

PADDINGTON   Good morning, Mr Gruber.

MR GRUBER   You've chosen a good time to call.

PADDINGTON   Have I?

MR GRUBER   Yes, it's just eleven o'clock. Time for buns and cocoa.

PADDINGTON   So it is! But I really came to ask you something. Mr Gruber, do you like parties?

MR GRUBER   Yes, I do, Mr Brown. I don't get invited to many nowadays, but I always enjoy them when I do.

PADDINGTON   Would you like to come to *my* party on Monday?

MR GRUBER   I'd be delighted. Is it your birthday?

PADDINGTON   Yes, it's my summer one.

MR GRUBER   Your summer one?

PADDINGTON   I have one in the winter as well. Bears have two birthdays every year, like the Queen.

MR GRUBER   I see. Well, I'll look forward to it very much indeed, Mr Brown. What time shall I come?

PADDINGTON   About four o'clock.

MR GRUBER   Right. I've got something in here which might come in useful. It isn't brand new, but it's very unusual. [*He brings a cardboard box from the back of the shop*] It's a conjuring set.

PADDINGTON   A conjuring set!

MR GRUBER   If you take it home with you today you'll have a chance to practise some of the tricks before Monday. Then you can entertain everybody at the party.

PADDINGTON   What a good idea. Thank you very much, Mr Gruber.

MR GRUBER   [*he opens the box*] There's a magic wand and a magic table which will help you to make things disappear. [*He sets it up*] Could you lend me your marmalade for a moment, Mr Brown?

PADDINGTON   [*looking in his case*] Here you are, Mr Gruber. There isn't very much left, I'm afraid. [*He hands the jar to* MR GRUBER]

MR GRUBER   That will do very well. [*He places the jar on the table and covers it with a cloth*] Now, I wave the wand thus and say the magic word Abracadabra! [*He lifts the cloth and the marmalade has disappeared – into the pocket in the cloth*]

PADDINGTON   [*amazed*] It's disappeared!

MR GRUBER   Exactly. [*He hands the wand to* PADDINGTON] Now, I'll just hold the cloth here, and if you say the magic word . . .

PADDINGTON   Marmalade!

MR GRUBER   No, not that! Abracadabra!

PADDINGTON   Abracadabra!

MR GRUBER   [*he lifts the cloth*] There we are . . . safely back again. [*He returns the jar of marmalade to* PADDINGTON]

PADDINGTON   That's very clever. How do you do it?

MR GRUBER   It's quite easy really. There's a secret compartment under the table, and the marmalade dropped into it while I was holding the cloth.

PADDINGTON   Are there some more tricks in the box, Mr Gruber?

MR GRUBER   Oh, yes, quite a lot. And there's a book of instructions. But you must follow them very carefully.

PADDINGTON   Thank you very much, Mr Gruber. And thank you for the cocoa. I'll see you on Monday. [*He goes, taking the box with him*]

MR GRUBER   Good day, Mr Brown. Don't forget, read the instructions carefully!

Scene Two

[*The Browns' sitting room.* MRS BIRD *is laying the table*]

MRS BROWN   Is everything ready, Mrs Bird?

MRS BIRD   Yes. [*Putting the candle on the cake*] Now, how many will there be? You and Mr Brown, Jonathan, Judy, and Paddington – that's five, then Mr Gruber and me, that's seven.

MRS BROWN   And Mr Curry.

MRS BIRD   Mr Curry! I didn't know he'd been invited.

MRS BROWN   He wasn't. He invited himself.

MRS BIRD   Just because there's a free tea. I expect he'll even complain about that. I think it's disgusting, taking the crumbs off a young bear's plate like that.

MRS BROWN   He'll have to look slippy if he expects to get any crumbs off Paddington's plate.

JUDY   [*coming in*] Fancy! He lives next door and he didn't even bother to wish Paddington many happy returns!

MRS BROWN   Perhaps he will when the party starts.

JONATHAN   [*coming in*] It's four o'clock, isn't anybody here yet?

[*A knock at the door as* MR GRUBER *arrives, closely followed by* MR CURRY]

MRS BROWN   There's somebody now.

PADDINGTON   It's all right, Mrs Bird, I'll go. [*He goes to let* MR GRUBER *in*] Hello, Mr Gruber. Hello, Mr Curry. Please come in.

MR GRUBER   Thank you, Mr Brown.

MR CURRY   Thank you, bear.

MRS BROWN   Hello, it's very kind of you both to come.

JONATHAN   Where's Dad?

MR BROWN   [*appearing from the kitchen*] Here I am. Hello, Mr Gruber. Good afternoon, Mr Curry.

MR GRUBER   Good afternoon.

MR BROWN   Well now, we all know why we're here.

PADDINGTON   Yes!

MR BROWN   Because it's Paddington's birthday.

JONATHAN   Hurrah!

[PADDINGTON *goes outside*]

MR BROWN   And now, before we light the candle and
              get down to the real business of the after-
              noon . . . I think Paddington has a surprise
              for us. He's going to do some conjuring.

              [PADDINGTON *returns, carrying the conjuror's table, wand,
              and his book of instructions*]

PADDINGTON   [*waving his wand for silence, after looking at his
              instruction book*) Ladies and gentlemen, my
              next trick is impossible.

MR CURRY   Your *next* trick, but you haven't done one
              yet!

PADDINGTON   [*ignoring the interruption*] For this trick I shall
              require an egg.

MRS BIRD   Oh dear! [*She goes off to get one*]

MRS BROWN   I feel sure something dreadful is going to
              happen.

JONATHAN   I wonder if he's got a rabbit inside his hat.

PADDINGTON   [*raises his hat and a small parcel falls out*] I
              don't think so. Only some marmalade
              sandwiches.

MRS BIRD   [*returns with a dummy egg*] Here you are,
              Paddington.

PADDINGTON   [*taking it with a slight bow*] Thank you, Mrs
              Bird. I now place the egg in the centre of
              my magic table and cover it with the cloth,
              so. [*To* JONATHAN] Now, sir, you're quite
              sure the egg is there?

JONATHAN   Absolutely sure.

PADDINGTON   Good. [*He waves his wand*] Abracadabra!
              [*He lifts the cloth and the egg has disappeared
              into the pocket at the back of the table*]

JONATHAN   That's very good!

JUDY   I wonder how he does it.

MR CURRY   It's quite easy really. It's all done by sleight of paw. Not bad though, for a bear. But can you bring it back again?

PADDINGTON   [putting the cloth back over the table] Abracadabra! Now, ladies and gentlemen, when I lift the cloth, you will see that the egg has returned. [He whisks away the cloth and is surprised to find a jar of marmalade instead] That's funny!

MR CURRY   Oh, yes. Very funny. Making us think you were going to find an egg and it was a jar of marmalade all the time!

MR GRUBER   Very good, Mr Brown. [They all clap]

PADDINGTON   [after taking a bow] Thank you. For my next trick I need a watch.

MR BROWN   [anxiously] Are you sure? Wouldn't anything else do?

PADDINGTON   [consulting the book] It says a watch.

MR CURRY   Here you are, bear, I'll lend you mine. Only it's very valuable, so look after it.

PADDINGTON   Thank you, Mr Curry. [He places it on the table] This is a very good trick. [He covers the watch with the cloth] Now, I take this hammer [He takes a hammer from the box] and I hit the watch with it, so! [He hammers the watch]

MR CURRY   [rising] I hope you know what you're doing, young bear.

PADDINGTON [*he hits it again*] Now, Mr Curry, perhaps you'll lift the cloth for me. [MR CURRY *lifts the cloth and sees his battered watch*]

MR CURRY What's this?

PADDINGTON Oh, dear! I think I forgot to say abracadabra.

MR CURRY Abracadabra! *Abracadabra!* [*He snatches up the remains of the watch*] Twenty years I've had this watch, and now look at it. Shockproof . . .

MR BROWN It doesn't look very shock-proof to me.

MR CURRY Seventeen jewels!

PADDINGTON [*he pretends to sweep up some remains and hands them to* MR CURRY] There are still some left, Mr Curry.

MR CURRY Pah!

MR GRUBER May I see that watch a moment? [*He examines it carefully*]

MR CURRY You may – what's left of it!

MR GRUBER There may not be much left, Mr Curry, but I know one of my own watches when I see it. You bought this from me for fifty pence not six months ago! You ought to be ashamed of yourself, telling lies like that in front of a young bear.

MR CURRY Rubbish! [He *sits down grumpily in the armchair and is horrified when he realizes that something very unpleasant has happened*] I'm sitting on something wet and sticky!

PADDINGTON   Oh dear, I expect it's my disappearing egg.
             It must have reappeared.

MR CURRY   [rising furiously] I've never been so insulted
             in my life. Never! [He points an accusing
             finger at the company] It's the last time I shall
             ever come to one of *your* birthday parties.
             [He storms out]

MRS BROWN   [as MR BROWN begins to laugh] Henry, you
             really oughtn't to laugh.

MR BROWN   It's no good, I can't help it.

MR GRUBER   [joining in] Did you see his face when all of
             the cogs fell out?

JONATHAN   And when Paddington gave him back his
             jewels?

JUDY   [imitating Paddington] There are still some
             left, Mr Curry. [By this time they are helpless
             with laughter]

MR GRUBER   I bet the man who invented that trick never
             saw it performed better.

PADDINGTON   I'm glad you enjoyed it. Would you like
             me to do some more?

MR BROWN   [hastily] No, thank you. The secret of success
             as an entertainer is to leave the audience
             wanting more.

MRS BIRD   [lighting the candle] I suggest we see if we
             can make that cake disappear instead.

JUDY   Now, Paddington, you must blow out the
             candle and make a wish.

PADDINGTON   I wish . . .

JONATHAN   No, you mustn't tell your wish to anybody.

PADDINGTON   All right. I wish [*He thinks a wish*] I wish . . .
             [*He blows out the candle*]

MR GRUBER   Happy Birthday, Mr Brown. [*They all cheer*]

PADDINGTON   Yes, it is. A very happy birthday.

JONATHAN   I've an idea. Let's all sing Happy Birthday. Are you ready?

ALL   Yes.

JONATHAN   Here we go then.

ALL   Happy Birthday to you,
             Happy Birthday to you,
             Happy Birthday dear Paddington,
             Happy Birthday to you.

[*They cheer as the play ends*]

CURTAIN

Paddington Visits the Dentist

CAST OF CHARACTERS

MRS BROWN

MR BROWN

JUDY

JONATHAN

MRS BIRD

PADDINGTON

MR LEACH, the dentist

NURSE

PROPS

At the Browns' house:
Chairs and table
Plates

At the dentist's surgery:
Chair
Table
Scarf
Glass of orange squash
Tray for dentist's instruments
Metal ballpoint pen for syringe
*Toy false teeth
Large piece of chewing gum or soft sweet
Paper bag of sweets
Small brush
Two white coats

The Browns' dining room at Number thirty-two, Windsor Gardens is not very different from their sitting room. A table and chairs are all that is necessary. For Mr Leach's surgery we will require a chair for PADDINGTON to sit in when his teeth are examined, a beaker of orange squash (in place of mouthwash), a small metal ballpoint pen (for the syringe) and a model of *Mr Leach's teeth stuck in toffee and concealed in his coat pocket before the play starts. These can be toy teeth or made from plasticine. MR LEACH and the NURSE should both wear white coats over their clothes.

Scene One

[*The Browns' dining room. The Browns have just finished breakfast and* JUDY *and* JONATHAN *are helping to clear away.*]

MRS BROWN   We shall never hear the last of it. I'm sure of that.

MR BROWN   [*as he enters*] What's that, Mary?

MRS BROWN   Paddington's tooth. It's been put into the waste disposal unit by mistake.

JUDY   And he wanted to keep it to put under his pillow, so that he would find five pence in the morning. He's very upset.

MR BROWN   Well, he could try leaving a note under his pillow explaining what happened.

JUDY   Perhaps it would be worth looking under the drain cover. It might still be there.

JONATHAN   I shouldn't think so. Those waste disposals are very good. They grind up everything.

MRS BROWN   I don't think he's lost a tooth at all, I think he broke a piece off when he was testing his everlasting toffee.

MR BROWN   Whatever is everlasting toffee?

MRS BIRD   You may well ask. It's something Paddington invented yesterday. It set so hard it took me two hours to get it off the saucepan.

PADDINGTON   [*offstage*] Ooooh!

MR BROWN   What are we going to do about him?

MRS BIRD   I've arranged an appointment with the dentist. Mr Leach is seeing him this morning.

PADDINGTON [*enters*] Ooooh!

MR BROWN I'm sorry to hear you've lost your tooth, Paddington.

PADDINGTON Yes. I've had it ever since I was born and I've cleaned it twice every day. I don't know what Aunt Lucy's going to say when I tell her.

MRS BROWN Let's worry about that later. Mrs Bird has made an appointment with Mr Leach.

PADDINGTON Mr Leach?

MRS BROWN Our dentist. I'm sure he'll soon put you right. He's been practising for years.

PADDINGTON Mr Leach has been *practising*? I think I'd sooner pay extra and have somebody who knows what he's doing . . .

Scene Two

[*Mr Leach's surgery.* MR LEACH *is talking to his* NURSE]

MR LEACH Who have we first today, Miss Kay?

NURSE Mrs Brown, sir. An emergency appointment.

[*She goes through the surgery door and ushers in* MRS BROWN *and* PADDINGTON, *wearing a scarf tied round his head and under his chin*]

MR LEACH Good morning, Mrs Brown.

MRS BROWN Good morning, Mr Leach.

MR LEACH Now, what can I do for you?

MRS BROWN It's Paddington. He's having trouble with a tooth.

61

MR LEACH   Hmm. Well, I'm afraid I shall have to charge extra. Bears have forty-two teeth.

PADDINGTON   I've only got forty-one. One of mine's been disposed of.

MR LEACH   That's still nine more than I usually deal with. I shall have to get my nurse to draw up a completely new chart. Now, perhaps you'll sit yourself down there. [*He ushers* PADDINGTON *into the chair and then goes round the back.* PADDINGTON *jumps out of the chair and hurries round the back in order to see what's going on. As he does so,* MR LEACH *comes round the front*]

MR LEACH   Where is he? Nurse, what's happened to my patient?

NURSE   He was here a moment ago.

[*They both go round the back of the chair just as* PADDINGTON *comes round to the front again*]

PADDINGTON   [*settling down*] Here I am, Mr Leach. [*He removes his scarf, opens his mouth and points to it*] It's in here. At least, it was!

MR LEACH   I can see this is going to be one of those days. [*He examines Paddington's teeth, peering into his mouth*] Say aah!

PADDINGTON   Aaah . . .

MR LEACH   [*he feels a tooth with his finger*] Mmm. Mmmmmm. Uh, huh.

PADDINGTON   [*copying*] Mm. Mmmmmm. Uh, huh.

[*This can be repeated if it gets a laugh*]

MR LEACH   [*breathing heavily as he gives up*] I think that will be enough, thank you.

PADDINGTON   [*standing up*] Thank *you*, Mr Leach. That didn't hurt at all.

MR LEACH   I haven't done anything yet. That was only an inspection – just to see what's what. We've a long way to go yet, I'm afraid. You have what is known as a fractured cusp.

PADDINGTON   A fractured cusp! It was all right when I came in. You must have poked it with your finger.

MR LEACH   A fractured cusp simply means that you have a broken tooth. You have quite a large piece missing.

PADDINGTON   Oh, dear! I think I'd like a glass of orangeade. [*He goes to drink the mouthwash*]

MR LEACH   That is *not* orangeade. It's put there for patients to use afterwards.

PADDINGTON   [*hands the beaker to the* NURSE] I'm very sorry, Patience, I didn't know it was yours. There's still some left.

NURSE   Thank you. [*Takes the beaker and starts to drink*]

MR LEACH   Nurse! [*He picks up the syringe*] Now, we're going to have something to take our mind off your tooth.

PADDINGTON   You mean, a bun?

MR LEACH   No, an injection. Open wide. [*He gives* PADDINGTON *the injection*] There! That didn't hurt, did it?

PADDINGTON Not at all, thank you. [*He stands up and takes the syringe*] Shall I give you yours now?

MR LEACH [*jumps back*] Mine! *I* don't have an injection.

PADDINGTON But you said *we* were going to have something to take *our* mind off *my* tooth.

MR LEACH Nurse! I think we'll try taking a wax impression. It may make things easier . . . and quieter.

NURSE Yes, sir. [*She hands him a piece of "wax", which could be a large piece of chewing gum or other soft sweet*]

MR LEACH Now, I want you to open your mouth again, say "ah" and when I've put this in, take a good, hard bite.

PADDINGTON Aaaaah!

MR LEACH Good. Now, one more "ah" like that. And whatever happens from now on – don't let go.

PADDINGTON Aaaaah! [*He bites on the "wax", trapping Mr Leach's thumb*]

MR LEACH Ooooooooh!

PADDINGTON Ooooooooh!

MR LEACH Owwwwwwwwwww!

PADDINGTON Owwwwwwwwwww!

MR LEACH Let go!

[PADDINGTON *shakes his head*]
Help, somebody!

MRS BROWN   Oh, dear. Nurse, you grab Mr Leach. I'll pull Paddington.

[*There is a tremendous tug of war. Finally* PADDINGTON *lets go and* MR LEACH *and the* NURSE *fall over*]

MR LEACH   Why didn't you let go?

PADDINGTON   You told me not to. You said bite hard and don't let go, whatever happens. [*He hands* MR LEACH *the "wax"*]

MR LEACH   [*examines it*] I wanted an impression of your teeth – not my thumb!

MRS BROWN   Mr Leach, would you like us to come back another day?

MR LEACH   [*bravely*] No. No, I'll just paint your tooth with this liquid to stop it from hurting. [*he does this*] And if you'll come back next week, I'll give you a nice, new, gold tooth to replace the one that's missing.

PADDINGTON   [*delighted*] A *gold* tooth! I shall keep it for Sundays . . . I shan't eat with it.

MR LEACH   Er . . . yes.

MRS BROWN   That sounds splendid.

PADDINGTON   Thank you very much, Mr Leach. It's very kind of you. [*He offers him a paper bag*] Perhaps you'd like to try one of these?

MR LEACH   I . . . er . . . I don't normally eat toffees. It doesn't set a very good example. But I must say they look rather tempting. [*He helps himself*] It's most kind of you. [*He chews on one of Paddington's everlasting toffees*] It's really very good . . . [*His jaws stick together*] Grrr! Glug!

PADDINGTON   I'm glad you like it, Mr Leach. It's a new kind of toffee I've just invented. They're everlasting.

[MR LEACH *staggers about the surgery, trying to open his jaws. When he eventually succeeds, he pretends to remove a large lump of toffee from his mouth. There is what looks like a set of false teeth embedded in it. He holds it up for everybody to see and points to the teeth. From now on he has to pretend he has no teeth*]

MR LEACH   My teeth! [*He collapses into the chair*] Look at them! [*He puts the teeth down on the instrument tray*]

PADDINGTON   I think perhaps you've fractured your cusps, Mr Leach. If you open your mouth, I'll soon put it right for you. [*He picks up the syringe*]

MR LEACH   [*opens his mouth and then realizes what he is doing*] Oh, no, you don't! [*He rushes out*]

PADDINGTON   Oh, dear. I was looking forward to being a dentist. [*He advances hopefully towards the* NURSE]

NURSE   [*hastily leaving the room too*] No, thank you very much.

MRS BROWN   Come along, Paddington. [*She makes to leave*]

PADDINGTON   [*examines Mr Leach's teeth with interest*] What a waste of good toffee. On the other hand, it's a good idea having detachable teeth. [*He follows* MRS BROWN *off*] If everyone had detachable teeth, there wouldn't be any need for dentists . . .

CURTAIN

Paddington Goes to the Launderette

CAST OF CHARACTERS

MRS BIRD

PADDINGTON

LAUNDERETTE ATTENDANT

MR GRUBER

MR CURRY

PROPS

Sheet of paper for list

Three laundry bags or pillowcases (two for Mrs Bird, one for Mr Gruber)

A pile of laundry – rags or old clothes

Pair of socks (normal size)

Pair of "shrunken" socks (baby size)

Pair of long combinations

*Pair of long combinations – enormously long

A few coins

Small packet (Paddington's sandwich)

Wheelbarrow

Four paper cups

Sign with instructions

*Three big cardboard boxes – two to be washing machines, one for the cocoa machine

Soap powder

Tray

Chairs

Magazine

Piece of wet bread (Paddington's soggy sandwich)

This is probably the most difficult play in the book and will need plenty of rehearsal if everything is to work at the right time. *Two cardboard packing cases with flaps cut into the tops will do for the washing machines. One of these boxes will have to be big enough for someone to hide inside. This person will have to throw out a soggy sandwich (p. 74) without being seen. If possible, there should be some sort of sound effect when the washing machine turns on (p. 73). This could be water sloshing in a bucket or a mechanical noise.

A third box will be needed for the cocoa machine, and this should be big enough to hide the person who will push the cocoa through an opening in the box. It should also have a coin slot. The two loud bangs can be made by thumping a tub or banging two tins together.

If you can't find a buzzer, a bicycle bell will do to sound the washing machine alarm, but the more noise the better! *Mr Curry's "stretched" long combinations could be cut from a sheet. They and the "shrunken" socks should be hidden in the washing machines before the play begins.

Instructions can be painted on cardboard and hung on the walls.

Scene One

[*The Browns' sitting room.* MRS BIRD *is putting two piles of washing into bags and checking them against a list*]

MRS BIRD   Four pairs of socks, two woollen vests, one pair of long combinations . . .

PADDINGTON [*enters*] Hullo, Mrs Bird.

MRS BIRD   Two shirts, four pillowcases, and one table-cloth. Hullo, Paddington. I must hurry, I want to catch the laundry man.

PADDINGTON I'm afraid it's too late, Mrs Bird. He's already been. He went down the street about ten minutes ago.

MRS BIRD   There now! I asked him to call, he must have forgotten. Now what shall I do? These things *must* be washed today.

PADDINGTON Would you like me to take them to the launderette, Mrs Bird?

MRS BIRD   I don't know. Launderettes are rather complicated.

PADDINGTON I'm sure I could manage. Mr Gruber's told me about them. He says you just put the clothes in the machines, and then you sit and watch them going round and round. He says it's better than watching television.

MRS BIRD   Well, beggars can't be choosers, I suppose. I've got some of Mr Curry's things to take as well. He left them for the laundry man. Some socks and his long combinations.

PADDINGTON I don't mind taking Mr Curry's clothes.

MRS BIRD   Are you sure you can manage?

PADDINGTON   Quite sure, Mrs Bird.

MRS BIRD   Well, here's some money. [*She hands it to him*] You'll find there's a cocoa machine in the launderette: if you put five pence into the slot, you'll get a good hot cup of cocoa so you can have your elevenses while the clothes are being washed.

PADDINGTON   Thank you very much, Mrs Bird.

MRS BIRD   And perhaps you would like to take this as well. [*She hands him a sandwich*]

PADDINGTON   [*putting it inside his hat*] Thank you, Mrs Bird.

MRS BIRD   Thank *you*, Paddington.

Scene Two

[*The launderette. The* ATTENDANT *puts down her magazine as* PADDINGTON *comes through the door. He has the washing loose in a wheelbarrow*]

ATTENDANT   Come in, dear. My, you look as if you've got the washing for the whole street!

PADDINGTON   Oh, no, it's for Mrs Bird.

ATTENDANT   *Mrs* Bird? [*She holds up Mr Curry's long combinations*]

PADDINGTON   Yes. And Mr Curry, of course. [*He gives her a look*]

ATTENDANT   Oh, of course!

PADDINGTON   What do I have to do?

ATTENDANT   I'm afraid you'll need two machines for this lot. I'll give you number eleven and number twelve. You do know how to work them?

PADDINGTON   I think so.

ATTENDANT   Well, if you get into any trouble, the instructions are on the wall. [*She places four beakers of detergent on a nearby tray*] That's two beakers for each machine. You put the first lot in when it starts and the second lot when the buzzer sounds.

PADDINGTON   Thank you very much.

[*The* ATTENDANT *exits.* MR GRUBER *enters and collects his washing*]

MR GRUBER   Why, hullo Mr Brown. I didn't expect to see you here.

PADDINGTON   Hello, Mr Gruber, I'm very pleased to see you.

MR GRUBER   I've come to collect my washing. Is anything the matter?

PADDINGTON   I'm not sure which bundle of washing should go in the hot wash and which in the warm wash.

MR GRUBER   Oh, I expect I can help you there. [*He examines the bundles*] All of these go into the hot wash, and this bundle goes into the warm wash. [*He places them carefully*] The bundle on the *left* goes in the hot, and this bundle on the *right* goes into the warm. That's easy to remember, isn't it?

PADDINGTON   Oh yes, thank you. Left, hot. Right, warm.

MR GRUBER   You must get it the right way round or some will shrink and the others will stretch.

PADDINGTON   Have you finished your washing for today?

MR GRUBER   Oh, yes. I'm just leaving. Perhaps you would like to drop in for elevenses on your way home?

PADDINGTON   It's very kind of you, Mr Gruber, but I expect I'll get some cocoa from the machine.

MR GRUBER   Well, I'll have to get along and open the shop.

PADDINGTON   Goodbye, Mr Gruber. I'll see you soon, I hope.

MR GRUBER   Yes, goodbye, Mr Brown.

[PADDINGTON *switches on the washing machines. The machine sound effects begin*]

PADDINGTON   Now, what did Mr Gruber say? Left, hot; right, warm. [*He walks over to the two bundles but looks at them from the other side so that left and right are reversed*] Left, hot. [*He puts it in the warm machine*] Right, warm. [*He puts the other bundle into the hot machine*] It's lucky that Mr Gruber came along. Now, what do I have to do? I know, put in one beaker of soap powder when the machine starts. [*He pours a carton of soap powder into the top of each machine*] That's right. Perhaps I'll have time for my elevenses before the buzzer sounds.

[*He crosses to the cocoa machine and puts a coin in the slot, but no cocoa appears*]

Oh, dear. It doesn't seem to be working.

[*He gives the machine a thump and immediately things start to happen. Cups of cocoa emerge through a hole in the front, one after another.* PADDINGTON *soon fills the tray, and they become mixed with the beakers of soap He tries to drink some in order to make room, but picks up a soap carton by mistake*]

       Ugh! Soap!

[*He picks up the tray but at that moment the buzzer sounds. He is so confused that he starts emptying beakers of cocoa into the washing machines. There are two loud bangs from the machines.* PADDINGTON *lifts the lid of one of the machines, removes his hat and tries to blow away the steam. In doing so, his marmalade sandwich falls into the wash. He leans over and peers into the machine as* MR CURRY *enters.* MR CURRY *crosses and peers into the machine too*]

MR CURRY   Bear! What are you doing, bear?

[PADDINGTON *jumps out of the way and as he does so, something white and doughy flies out of the washing machine and hits* MR CURRY *in the face*]

       Ugh! [*He wipes it off*] What on earth is this?

PADDINGTON   I think it's a marmalade sandwich, Mr Curry. I dropped one in by mistake.

MR CURRY   A marmalade sandwich? In a washing machine? Whatever next? And what's happened to my laundry? I heard you were doing it and I've come down to make sure it's all right.

PADDINGTON   I think it's ready now, Mr Curry. [*He opens the lid of the first machine*] Here are your socks.

[*He presents* MR CURRY *with the smallest pair of socks imaginable*]

MR CURRY   My *socks*? Look at them! They've shrunk. If you've done the same thing to my combinations, bear, I'll . . . I'll . . .

PADDINGTON   Oh, I don't think so, Mr Curry. They were in a different machine. [*He opens the door of the second machine*]

MR CURRY   Disgraceful! Give them here.
[*He grabs the ankles of the combinations as* PADDINGTON *pulls them out. They are now ten times as long as they were before. As* MR CURRY *spins across the launderette, they wrap themselves round him until he looks like an Egyptian mummy*]

PADDINGTON   You see, Mr Curry. I told you they wouldn't have shrunk.

MR CURRY   [*helpless*] Bear! Are you trying to take me for a ride?

PADDINGTON   [*comes up behind him with the wheelbarrow*] Take you for a ride? Certainly, Mr Curry!
[MR CURRY *falls over backwards into the wheelbarrow and is carried off at high speed by* PADDINGTON]

CURTAIN

Paddington Goes to the Hospital

CAST OF CHARACTERS

MRS BROWN
MRS BIRD
PADDINGTON
NURSE
MR HEINZ, the psychiatrist
SIR ARCHIBALD, the doctor
MR CURRY

PROPS

In the Browns' sitting room:
Chairs, table, etc.
Thermos
Basket
Fruit
*Cake with cherries on top
Letter
Paddington's hat

In the hospital:
Desk or table
Chairs
Toy telephone
Sheet of paper for list
Doctor's bag (toy bag or old handbag)
containing toy stethoscope and
hand mirror
White overall
*Operating mask
Pushchair
Blanket
Box of toy tools – hammer, chisel, saw, *mallet
Three white coats

The first scene takes place in the Browns' sitting room. For the rest of the play we need a small table, with a toy telephone and two chairs. There should be a long white overall for PAD-DINGTON to wear when he dresses up as the doctor and *a handkerchief (with loops to hook round the ears) for the operating mask. Any simple box will do for the tools. *The mallet, used to frighten MR CURRY (p. 91), can be a toy mallet, but the bigger it is the funnier it will be. You could make a big mallet by attaching a large tin can to a broom handle. It is *not* to be used, of course! A strong pushchair could serve as Mr Curry's wheel-chair. The NURSE, SIR ARCHIBALD and MR HEINZ should wear white coats over their clothes.

PADDINGTON will also need a basket with some fruit, and if possible, a cake. *The cake doesn't have to be seen (it can stay in the basket), but if you do make one (real or imitation), be sure to put cherries on the top!

Scene One

[*The Browns' sitting room.* MRS BROWN *is making up a basket of food when* MRS BIRD *comes in*]

MRS BROWN   If I see another bunch of grapes I shall scream. That's the third this week. Not to mention four pots of jam, two dozen eggs and a jar of calves-foot jelly.

MRS BIRD   I thought Mr Curry was supposed to be ill. He seems to have a very healthy appetite.

MRS BROWN   He says he hurt his leg in the launderette the other day. I don't know how long he'll be in hospital.

MRS BIRD   If you ask me, Mr Curry will be coming out of hospital when it suits *him* and not a minute before. He knows when he is on to a good thing. Free board and lodging.

MRS BROWN   And everybody at his beck and call.

MRS BIRD   He has a relapse every time the doctor says he is getting better. The Ward Sister has given him some strong hints that they're short of beds, but he takes no notice. And I'm certainly not having him staying here.

[PADDINGTON *comes in carrying a letter*]

PADDINGTON   There's a letter for you, Mrs Brown. It looks like Mr Curry's writing.

MRS BROWN   Yes, I'm afraid you're right. [*She opens the envelope*]

MRS BIRD   What does he say?

MRS BROWN   [*reading*] Dear Mrs Brown, my leg is still troubling me. Will you please send some more apples. I didn't like the last lot – they were too sour. Also another cherry cake. P.S. Two cherries were missing from the one you sent last week.

PADDINGTON   [*guiltily*] Perhaps they were a bit loose?

MRS BIRD   [*with meaning*] Perhaps!

MRS BROWN   P.P.S. I would like them as soon as possible. Paddington could bring them round to the hospital . . . Do you mind taking this parcel to him, Paddington?

PADDINGTON   [*cheerfully*] No. I don't think I've ever been to a hospital before. I wonder if it's like the Daredevil Doctor series on television?

MRS BIRD   I shouldn't think so for one moment.

MRS BROWN   There now. It's packed. And I've fixed the cherries *firmly* in the cake this time, so let's hope they don't fall out.

MRS BIRD   I've packed you some sandwiches and a thermos flask of cocoa. But be careful, it's very hot.

PADDINGTON   Thank you Mrs Bird. I won't be long. [*He puts on his hat as he goes out*]

MRS BROWN   I do hope we're doing the right thing, letting him go by himself.

MRS BIRD   I shouldn't worry about that bear. He knows how to look after number one.

MRS BROWN   It wasn't Paddington I was thinking of, it's the hospital . . .

81

Scene Two

[*A small room in the hospital. A* NURSE *sits at the desk with a telephone. She is finishing a conversation*]

NURSE   Yes, Sir Archibald. Very good, Sir Archibald.

[*She replaces the phone as* PADDINGTON *knocks at the door*]

     Come in.

PADDINGTON   Good morning.

NURSE   Good morning. Can I help you?

PADDINGTON   I've come to see Mr Curry.

NURSE   [*looking through a list*] Mr Curry . . . have you any idea what he does?

PADDINGTON   He grumbles a lot.

NURSE   That doesn't help. I think I'd better pass you on to the person who deals with enquiries.

PADDINGTON   Thank you very much. Is he the head man?

NURSE   The *head* man. Bless me! Why didn't you say so before? You want the doctor who looks after things up here. [*She taps her head*]

PADDINGTON   Up here? [*He taps his own head*]

NURSE   Yes. He's what we call the head shrinker.

PADDINGTON   My hat *is* a bit tight. But I don't think I want my head shrunk. Couldn't you stretch my hat instead?

NURSE   Stretch your hat?

PADDINGTON	Yes. If it was a bit bigger I could carry more sandwiches in it.
NURSE	[leaning across the desk] Sandwiches?
PADDINGTON	[leaning across the desk so that they are nose-to-nose] Yes, but I would still have to find somewhere for my cocoa.
NURSE	[alarmed] There, there. There's nothing to worry about. [Picks up the phone quickly and dials a number] Mr Heinz, could you come quickly, please? There's a patient who needs you urgently. Thank you. [Replaces the phone]
PADDINGTON	Mr Heinz! I don't want to see Mr Heinz, I want to see Mr Curry. I've brought him one of Mrs Bird's cherry cakes.
NURSE	[soothingly] I think you'll find Mr Heinz much nicer. He'll soon take your worries away. [MR HEINZ enters] Oh, Mr Heinz, I'm so glad to see you. [She looks at PADDINGTON and taps her head] There's the patient. [She hurries out]
PADDINGTON	Patient? Have I got long to wait?
MR HEINZ	Oh, no, in fact I'll start right away. Just open your coat, please.
PADDINGTON	I'm sorry about the cherry cake.
MR HEINZ	[taking off his glasses and staring at PADDINGTON] You are sorry about the cherry cake?
PADDINGTON	Yes. I wish I could give you a slice but Mr Curry would only complain. I can give you one of my marmalade sandwiches.

83

MR HEINZ   [*a slight shudder*] No, thank you. Now, I'd
                 like to play a little game. It's really to test
                 your reactions. [*He sits down in a chair by
                 his desk*]

PADDINGTON   A game to test my reactions? I didn't know
                 I had any.

MR HEINZ   Oh, yes. [*He puts his feet up on another
                 chair*] Everybody has reactions. Some have
                 fast ones and some have slow. [PAD-
                 DINGTON *sits on his feet*] Oooh!

PADDINGTON   I'm sorry, Mr Heinz.

MR HEINZ   Now, I'm going to call out some words –
                 quite quickly – and each time I call one
                 out, I want you to give me another word
                 which has the opposite meaning . . .
                 right?

PADDINGTON   [*promptly, as he settles down in the other
                 chair*] Wrong.

MR HEINZ   What's the matter? Aren't you com-
                 fortable?

PADDINGTON   Oh, yes, but you told me to say the
                 opposite every time you gave me a
                 word.

MR HEINZ   That wasn't the word, bear! Wait until
                 I give you the go ahead. Once you start
                 I don't want to hear anything else.
                 Ready . . . Three . . . two . . . one . . . go!

PADDINGTON   Stop!

MR HEINZ   What's the matter?

PADDINGTON   You said "go" so I said "stop".

MR HEINZ	Oh. Very good.
PADDINGTON	Very bad.
MR HEINZ	Look here!
PADDINGTON	Look there! [*A pause*] Can't you think of any more words, Mr Heinz?
MR HEINZ	[*drums his fingers on the desk for a moment then decides to try again*] White.
PADDINGTON	Black.
MR HEINZ	Big.
PADDINGTON	Small.
MR HEINZ	Fast.
PADDINGTON	Slow.
MR HEINZ	Dark.
PADDINGTON	Light.
MR HEINZ	Fine.
PADDINGTON	Wet.
MR HEINZ	That's good. We've finished.
PADDINGTON	That's bad. We've started.
MR HEINZ	No, we haven't!
PADDINGTON	Yes, we have!
MR HEINZ	[*thumping table*] No . . . no . . . no!
PADDINGTON	[*thumps the table too, in his excitement*] Yes . . . yes . . . yes!
MR HEINZ	[*yelling*] Will you stop!
PADDINGTON	No, I won't!
MR HEINZ	[*his head in his hands*] Why did I ever take this up? I should have my head examined.

PADDINGTON   [*sitting up*] Perhaps it needs shrinking. I should go and talk to the nurse who was here a few minutes ago. She might be able to help you. She knows all about those things.

[*As* PADDINGTON *gets up,* MR HEINZ *makes a dash for the door*]

MR HEINZ   I shall be gone for five minutes. Five minutes! And if you're still here when I get back . . . I'll . . . I'll . . . [*He hurries out, at a loss for words*]

PADDINGTON   [*looking round the room*] What a funny hospital. It's not at all like the one in Daredevil Doctor. It must be time for elevenses. I'm glad Mrs Brown remembered to give me some cocoa. [*He fills the thermos cup and takes a mouthful*] Ow! [*He hops round the room in agony*] Ooh! [*He picks up a doctor's bag from the corner of the room, opens it and examines his tongue in a mirror*] I knew it, I've blistered my tongue . . . [*He becomes interested in the contents of the bag*] What's this? [*He puts on a stethoscope and listens to his own heart*] Hmm. I wonder what it's like to be a doctor.

[*He slips on a white gown and hangs the stethoscope round his neck*]

    [*As a television surgeon*] Nurse! Instruments ready? All right, bring in the patient. [*He puts on his operating mask and paces up and down*] Now this is serious . . .

[*The* NURSE *comes in suddenly*]

NURSE   It certainly is serious. Sir Archibald is
                   coming.

PADDINGTON   Is he?

NURSE   And he's in a terrible mood. You know he
                   doesn't like students who aren't punctual.

PADDINGTON   Student? But I'm not . . .

NURSE   He's here now. I'd say I'm sorry straight
                   away, if I were you.

SIR ARCHIBALD   [*storming in*] Ah, there you are.

PADDINGTON   Good morning, Sir Archibald. I'm sorry,
                   Sir Archibald!

SIR ARCHIBALD   Sorry? I should think so! Good after-
                   noon's more like it! Now you *are* here,
                   perhaps you can give us the benefit of
                   your advice. I'd like to have your diag-
                   nosis.

PADDINGTON   My diagnosis! [*He begins to unload his
                   basket*] There's a cherry cake, some eggs,
                   some calves-foot jelly, but I don't think
                   Mrs Brown packed a diagnosis.

SIR ARCHIBALD   Calves-foot jelly. Did you say *calves-foot
                   jelly*?

PADDINGTON   Yes. Grant Dexter says it's very good if
                   you're ill.

SIR ARCHIBALD   Grant Dexter! And who might he be?

PADDINGTON   You don't know Grant Dexter? He's the
                   Daredevil Doctor. He's very good at
                   curing people. All his patients get better.

SIR ARCHIBALD   Are you suggesting mine don't, doctor
                   . . . whatever your name is?

87

PADDINGTON   Doctor? I'm not a doctor, Sir Archibald. [*He pulls off his mask*] I'm a bear. I've come to visit Mr Curry.

SIR ARCHIBALD   [*on the point of exploding*] Curry? Did you say Curry?

PADDINGTON   That's right.

SIR ARCHIBALD   Are you a friend of his?

PADDINGTON   Well, I'm not really a friend. He lives next door and I've brought him some food to be going on with.

SIR ARCHIBALD   Food! That's the last thing he needs. It will only make him stay longer. That man's entirely without scruples.

PADDINGTON   Mr Curry's without scruples! I thought he'd only hurt his leg!

SIR ARCHIBALD   Scruples, bear, are things that stop some people taking advantage of others.

PADDINGTON   Oh. I don't think Mr Curry's got any of those, Sir Archibald. Mrs Bird's always grumbling because he takes advantage of others.

SIR ARCHIBALD   I see. [*Thoughtfully*] Are you any good at tricks, bear?

PADDINGTON   Oh, yes, Sir Archibald. Bears are very good at tricks.

SIR ARCHIBALD   I thought you might be. Nurse, wheel Mr Curry in here, we'll see him privately.

[*The* NURSE *goes and* SIR ARCHIBALD *turns to* PADDINGTON]

    I think it's time we gave Mr Curry a

surprise – and I think you're the one to give it. Now, if you'll just put your mask back on, bear . . .

PADDINGTON Yes, Sir Archibald. [*He does*]

SIR ARCHIBALD I'll give you a chance to see what it's like to be – what did you say his name was?

PADDINGTON Grant Dexter. The Daredevil Doctor.

SIR ARCHIBALD Now I've had an idea. [*He goes to the door and returns with a tool box*] The workmen left these when they were doing some repairs. When I tell you to get your instruments ready, this is the box I want you to take them from.

PADDINGTON Right, Sir Archibald.

[MR CURRY *arrives in a wheelchair pushed by the* NURSE]

SIR ARCHIBALD Good morning, Mr Curry.

MR CURRY [*overdoing the agony*] Oooooooh!

SIR ARCHIBALD How's the patient today?

MR CURRY Worse, much worse.

SIR ARCHIBALD [*cheerfully*] I thought you might be, that's why we have decided to operate.

MR CURRY [*sitting up quickly*] Operate? Did you say operate?

SIR ARCHIBALD Yes, that's right. No good playing around with these things. I'd like to introduce you to . . . a colleague from overseas. He specializes in legs. Does something or other to the knee. Nobody quite knows what, but it seems to work very well in the jungle. Quite a few of his patients

	still manage to get about after a fashion. [*To* PADDINGTON] Perhaps you'd like to listen to the patient's heart?
PADDINGTON	Of course, Sir Archibald. [*He sticks the stethoscope under the blanket*]
SIR ARCHIBALD	What can you hear?
PADDINGTON	It's got a very strong beat [*He jumps up and down to the rhythm*] I think it's Pick of the Pops.
MR CURRY	Pick of the Pops! You've got your stethoscope on my transistor radio!
PADDINGTON	I'm sorry, Mr Curry. [*In his confusion he reverses the stethoscope and puts the head-piece on* MR CURRY. *He shouts in the other end*] Are you there?

[MR CURRY *jumps*]

MR CURRY	Of course I am! [*He turns to* SIR ARCHIBALD] Is this . . . this *person* going to be allowed to operate on me? He's not big enough for a start.
SIR ARCHIBALD	[*calmly*] Oh, don't worry about his size. We'll give him a box to stand on.
MR CURRY	A box to stand on!
SIR ARCHIBALD	Yes, it may make him a bit wobbly but it'll be all right.
MR CURRY	What!
SIR ARCHIBALD	[*he turns to* PADDINGTON *with a wink*] Now, if you would just like to get your instruments ready.

PADDINGTON	Certainly, Sir Archibald. [*He opens the carpenter's tool box*] One hammer ... [*He puts it on the desk*]
MR CURRY	A hammer!
PADDINGTON	One chisel. [*He puts it next to the hammer*]
MR CURRY	A chisel!
PADDINGTON	And one saw. [*He brings out a large carpenter's saw*]
MR CURRY	A saw!
SIR ARCHIBALD	How about something to put him to sleep with, nurse?

[*The NURSE hands PADDINGTON an enormous mallet*]

MR CURRY	I'm off. [*He leaps out of the chair*]
SIR ARCHIBALD	Ah, Mr Curry, I'm glad you're feeling better. You can leave the hospital today.
MR CURRY	Leave? I don't know what you're talking about.
SIR ARCHIBALD	You aren't limping any more, Mr Curry. In fact, I would say you are completely cured.
MR CURRY	[*realizes he's been beaten*] Bah! [*He storms out*]
SIR ARCHIBALD	[*after his laughter has subsided*] It seems we have another free bed in the ward after all, nurse. [*He removes Paddington's mask and shakes his paw warmly*] Congratulations, bear. I've never in all my life seen a patient recover so quickly. Perhaps you would like to keep your stethoscope as a souvenir?

PADDINGTON Thank you very much, Sir Archibald. [*He picks up his basket*] Would you like some of this cake? I don't suppose Mr Curry will be needing it now.

SIR ARCHIBALD Mmm. It does seem rather a pity to waste it. [*He looks over his shoulder to make sure the nurse can't hear and then lowers his voice*] Do you like the cherries?

PADDINGTON [*lowers his voice too*] I think they're the best part. Except Mrs Bird's put them on extra tightly this time.

SIR ARCHIBALD [*reaches for the tool box*] I don't doubt we'll find something to lever them off with. [*He hands* PADDINGTON *a suitable tool*] After you . . .

PADDINGTON No, after you, Sir Archibald.

[*Together, they dig into the basket*]

CURTAIN

Paddington Turns Detective

CAST OF CHARACTERS

MR BROWN

MRS BROWN

MRS BIRD

PADDINGTON

MR GRUBER

POLICEMAN

MR CURRY

JUDY

JONATHAN

PROPS

In the Browns' sitting room:
Table, chairs, etc.
Paddington's hat
Torch
Sandwich
Plastic clothes line
Battery
Pillowcase
Lantern

In Mr Gruber's shop:
Chairs, bric–a–brac, etc.
Book
Cardboard box containing a magnifying glass, whistle, some small bottles, a pad of paper, and a false beard (could be made of yarn or cotton wool)
Large old coat

At Paddington Station:
Luggage and parcels
"Paddington Station" sign
Jar of marmalade
Photo–frame with picture of Aunt Lucy (with glass, if possible)

For the best effect this play needs to be performed after dark, or at least with the curtains drawn. Much of the action takes place at midnight, outside the Browns' house. It should not be necessary to change the scene: simply use the back part of the stage for the sitting room and the front part for the out-of-doors scene. This scene will be funnier if the BROWNS and MRS BIRD appear in their nightclothes – but this is a matter of choice.

PADDINGTON will need a simple detective outfit (a beard, a magnifying glass and a whistle are the most important items) and MRS BROWN should have a torch battery, plastic clothes line and a sandwich ready to give him before he goes to his room. You will also need an alarm clock for sound effects. Paddington Station is exactly the same as we saw it when Paddington arrived in the first play p. 14. The station announcement can be made by somebody speaking loudly into a bucket or tin basin.

The POLICEMAN should wear something that looks like a uniform. He can wear a toy helmet, or one that has been made of cardboard with a milkbottle top for the badge. He also needs a notepad and pencil.

Scene One

[*The Browns' sitting room.* MR *and* MRS BROWN *are talking*]

MR BROWN   I can't think who would do a thing like that.

MRS BROWN   Nor can I, Henry, it's never happened before.

MR BROWN   I suppose it's too late to do anything about it now. It's very disappointing.

MRS BIRD   [*coming in from the kitchen*] What's the matter, Mr Brown?

MR BROWN   Someone's stolen my prize marrow.

MRS BIRD   When did that happen?

MR BROWN   I don't know for sure. It was there on Wednesday. They must have stolen it during the night.

MRS BIRD   [*after exchanging a look with Mrs Brown*] Well, you've got several more.

[PADDINGTON *comes in*]

MR BROWN   That isn't the point.

PADDINGTON   Good morning, everybody.

MRS BIRD   Good morning, Paddington.

PADDINGTON   Is anything the matter, Mr Brown?

MR BROWN   Somebody has stolen my prize marrow. I've several more, of course, but they'll never be ready in time for the show.

PADDINGTON   Oh, dear! I'm sorry to hear that, Mr Brown.

MR BROWN	It's the biggest I've ever grown. I felt I was sure to win a prize. I've a good mind to offer a reward to anybody who tracks down the culprit [*A thoughtful look comes into* PADDINGTON'S *eye and he makes for the door*]
MRS BROWN	Aren't you having any breakfast this morning, Paddington?
PADDINGTON	No, thank you, Mrs Brown. I want to see Mr Gruber about something.
MRS BROWN	What's that?
PADDINGTON	I'm not sure until I see him. [*He puts on his hat and goes*]
MR BROWN	*Now* what has he got on his mind?
MRS BIRD	I don't know, but I noticed a funny look came into his eyes when you mentioned a reward . . .

Scene Two

[*Mr Gruber's shop.* MR GRUBER *puts down the book he is reading as* PADDINGTON *comes in*]

PADDINGTON	Good morning, Mr Gruber.
MR GRUBER	Good morning, Mr Brown. You're early today. It's only ten o'clock.
PADDINGTON	Yes. I've got a problem and I wondered if you could help me.
MR GRUBER	I'll do my best. Tell me about it.
PADDINGTON	It's a flashing light.
MR GRUBER	A flashing light?

PADDINGTON In the garden at Number thirty-two, Windsor Gardens – and Mr Brown's marrow.

MR GRUBER You'd better begin at the beginning.

PADDINGTON Yes, I suppose I had. You see, I've got a new torch and last night, when I was in bed, I shone it at the window by mistake. Then I noticed that somebody was flashing a light outside in the garden – like a signal. So I flashed my light on and off three times and the light outside the window flashed three times as well.

MR GRUBER What did you do?

PADDINGTON I pulled the bedclothes over my head and went to sleep!

MR GRUBER I see.

PADDINGTON Then, when I came down to breakfast this morning, Mr Brown told me that somebody had stolen his prize marrow.

MR GRUBER And you think that the two things are connected?

PADDINGTON That's right, and I thought I would like to catch whoever it is. Not just for the reward . . .

MR GRUBER [twinkling] Oh, there's a reward, is there?

PADDINGTON [casually] Mr Brown did mention it. Do you remember that book you showed me once about the famous detective?

MR GRUBER Sherlock Holmes? Yes.

PADDINGTON I would like to be able to catch criminals like he did. But I may need to disguise myself. It'll make things a lot easier.

MR GRUBER   I think I can help you there, Mr Brown. [*He takes down a cardboard box*] Somebody sold this to me a long time ago. You can borrow it if you like.

PADDINGTON [*reading from the lid of the box*] Master Detective's Disguise Outfit. Thank you very much, Mr Gruber. May I look inside?

MR GRUBER   Of course.

PADDINGTON It looks very interesting. [*He takes out a magnifying glass*] What's this, Mr Gruber?

MR GRUBER   That's a magnifying glass to look for clues.

PADDINGTON Very useful. And here's a police-whistle and some bottles and a pad.

MR GRUBER   They're for fingerprints and one of the bottles is full of invisible ink.

PADDINGTON And a beard! Just what I need.

MR GRUBER   Here. Try this old coat. It may be a bit big. [PADDINGTON *slips it on. It trails behind him*]

PADDINGTON Thank you very much, Mr Gruber. [*He hooks the beard over his ears*] How's that?

MR GRUBER   Splendid!

PADDINGTON [*putting his bush hat on*] I don't think anybody will recognize me now.

MR GRUBER   [*as Doctor Watson*] Do you think it will be a difficult crime to solve, Mr Holmes?

PADDINGTON On the contrary, elementary, my dear Watson. [*He tucks the disguise outfit under his arm and sails out*]

Scene Three

[*The living room at Number thirty-two, Windsor Gardens. There is a knock on the door.* MRS BIRD *goes to answer it*]

PADDINGTON [*in a deep voice*] Good morning.

MRS BIRD Oh, hello, Paddington. I didn't expect you back so quickly.

PADDINGTON I'm not Paddington, Mrs Bird. I'm Sherlock Holmes – the famous detective.

MRS BIRD Yes dear. Don't forget to wipe your feet.

MRS BROWN [*coming in from the kitchen*] Is Paddington back already? I thought he would be having his elevenses with Mr Gruber.

MRS BIRD He's up to something, but I don't know what. He's just come back in a long over-coat, hidden behind a beard like Father Christmas, and he looked very thoughtful.

MRS BROWN Oh, dear! Something always happens when he's like that.

[PADDINGTON *enters minus his disguise*]

PADDINGTON Hullo, Mrs Brown.

MRS BROWN Hallo, Paddington.

PADDINGTON I wonder if I could have a new battery for my torch?

MRS BROWN Is the other one flat already?

PADDINGTON Yes. I've had to use it rather a lot lately.

MRS BROWN Here you are.

PADDINGTON Thank you very much, Mrs Brown. [*He goes into the hall*]

MRS BIRD   I wonder why he needs his torch? [PAD-
                  DINGTON *comes back suddenly, making them
                  jump*]

PADDINGTON   Mrs Brown, do you happen to have some
                  rope I could borrow?

MRS BROWN   I don't think I have any rope but I've a
                  plastic clothes line. Would that be any
                  good?

PADDINGTON   [*gravely*] That would do very well.

MRS BIRD   Here you are. [*Gives him the clothes line*]

PADDINGTON   Thank you. [*He goes into the hall again*]

MRS BIRD   And what does he need those things for?

MRS BROWN   I shudder to think.

PADDINGTON   [*coming back suddenly again*] There's just
                  one more thing.

MRS BIRD   [*wearily*] Yes, Paddington?

PADDINGTON   I wonder if I could take my elevenses to my
                  room today. I'm not very hungry at the
                  moment, and I may feel like a marmalade
                  sandwich later.

MRS BROWN   Here you are, all ready and waiting for you.
                  [*She hands him the sandwiches on a plate*]

PADDINGTON   Thank you very much. [*He goes off as
                  MRS BROWN and MRS BIRD shake their heads
                  in amazement. After a moment they go off too*]

                  [*Blackout. After a moment the alarm clock sounds in the
                  distance*]

                  [PADDINGTON *yawns as he enters*] Midnight,
                  that's the best time to catch criminals.

[*He switches on his torch and shines it through the window*] Nothing there, but I'd better be prepared. [*He puts on his beard, overcoat and hat and picks up his case*] I'll go and hide in the greenhouse. [*He goes off. A moment later, a shadowy figure appears at the front of the stage. He is carrying a lantern, but is muffled up in a scarf so we don't see his face. As he reaches the front door,* PADDINGTON *comes along carrying the clothes line and pillowcase. The figure walks away and* PADDINGTON *creeps up behind him. The figure turns round suddenly, but* PADDINGTON *ducks and isn't noticed. The next time the figure turns away,* PADDINGTON *seizes his opportunity, pops the pillowcase and lassoo over his head and runs round him with the clothes line, pinning his arms to his sides so that he can't remove the pillowcase. When he is secured,* PADDINGTON *blows his whistle*]
It's no good struggling. You've met your match! [*The figure answers with a muffled snort and struggles to get free*] Be quiet, you will have your chance to speak when the police get here.

[PADDINGTON *leads him indoors just as the* POLICEMAN *arrives on the scene*]

POLICEMAN   Hullo. Hullo. What's going on here?

PADDINGTON   Good evening, Officer, that was quick.

POLICEMAN   I just happened to be passing, sir, and I heard your whistle. What's the trouble?

PADDINGTON   I've captured a burglar! I think he's the one who took Mr Brown's marrow.

POLICEMAN   Mr Brown's marrow?

PADDINGTON   That's right. I thought I saw a flashing light. Then I saw a shadowy figure. I couldn't see his face but from the way he walked, I'm sure it had a nasty look on it.

POLICEMAN   Well sir, let's see, shall we? I'll switch the light on. [*He switches on the light and then jerks the rope which* PADDINGTON *has been holding. The figure spins round until he comes to the end of it. The* POLICEMAN *undoes the lassoo and the figure wrenches the pillowcase from his head*]

PADDINGTON   Oh, dear! [*He puts his torch down*]

MR CURRY   What is the meaning of this assault?

POLICEMAN   [*to* PADDINGTON] You were right. He *has* got a nasty look on his face. You are accused of acting in a suspicious manner.

MR CURRY   Suspicious manner! I was going about my own business.

POLICEMAN   At midnight? With a lantern?

MR CURRY   I happen to collect moths and the light of the lantern attracts them. [*He suddenly sees* PADDINGTON] Bear! I might have known you would be at the bottom of this.

PADDINGTON   I'm sorry, Mr Curry. [*He takes off his beard*]

MR CURRY   Not as sorry as you will be!

POLICEMAN   Hmmm. And what were you doing prowling round the house in disguise, young fellow-me-bear?

[MR *and* MRS BROWN, *awakened by the din, come onstage*]

POLICEMAN Unless you can explain yourself . . .

MR BROWN Whatever is the matter?

PADDINGTON Well, I'm afraid it's a bit complicated. You see, it all happened because of your marrow, Mr Brown . . . The one you were getting ready for the show. I was trying to catch the thief.

MR BROWN I don't see how my marrow has anything to do with this noise.

MRS BROWN I think I'm beginning to understand . . . Paddington was trying to catch the person who took it. But I'm afraid he didn't stand a chance.

POLICEMAN Why not, madam?

MRS BROWN I was going to tell you sooner or later, Henry. It's my fault really, you see . . . I cut your marrow by mistake!

MR BROWN You did? You cut my prize marrow?

MRS BROWN Well, I didn't realize it was your prize one. And you know how fond you are of stuffed marrow. We had it for dinner on Thursday.

MR BROWN We had it for dinner? How could you?

POLICEMAN Here, not so fast, sir, I can't get it all down. Has anybody else anything to say?

MR CURRY Yes, I have. I demand that this bear is punished. Springing out on an innocent member of the public. I shall demand damages. [PADDINGTON *is very unhappy at the trouble that he has caused. He decides to creep quietly away before anybody notices*]

POLICEMAN	[*to* MR BROWN] What do you say to that, sir?
MR BROWN	As my marrow seems to have caused all this trouble, perhaps I had better try to find a solution to the problem. This morning I promised a reward to anybody who found out who took the marrow. Now, through you, Mr Curry, we have actually found the culprit. [MRS BROWN *looks guilty*] Suppose I gave the reward to *you*. Would that satisfy you?
MR CURRY	Well, I don't know . . .
MR BROWN	Say five pounds?
MR CURRY	[*after a moment's hesitation*] Very well, but it mustn't happen again. And I demand an apology.
MR BROWN	I'm sure Paddington didn't mean any harm, but, of course, he will apologize.
MRS BROWN	Where is he?

[JUDY *and* JONATHAN, *who have appeared by this time, begin to look for him*]

MRS BIRD	[*enters*] Whatever is going on here?
JUDY	It's Paddington. He's missing.
JONATHAN	He isn't in his room. I've just looked in there.
JUDY	And all his things have gone.
JONATHAN	His suitcase . . .
JUDY	His clothes . . . and his picture of Aunt Lucy . . .
JONATHAN	Everything!

MRS BROWN   Where on earth can he have got to?

MR BROWN   There's only one thing for it, we must organize a search party. [*He picks up the torch*]

MRS BROWN   But where can we look? We don't even know where to start.

MRS BIRD   [*grimly, as she puts on her coat*] I do . . . follow me. If you want my opinion, there isn't a moment to lose.

[MRS BIRD *hurries out followed by the rest of the family*]

MR CURRY   Hey! Hold on! Wait for me! [*He hurries after them*]

Scene Four

[*Paddington Station. It is set as in the first play, p. 15, with luggage and parcels. There is an announcement over the tannoy "The train about to leave from Platform One is the Boat-train Special". A Guard's whistle sounds. The* BROWNS *rush across stage, but the train is already moving off. A moment later they walk sadly back on*]

JUDY   Too late!

MR BROWN   We don't *know* he was on it.

JONATHAN   I bet he was. I bet Mrs Bird was right.

JUDY   She usually is. Besides, you heard what they said . . .

JONATHAN   It was the Boat-train Special!

MRS BROWN   Goodness knows where he'll end up.

MRS BIRD   [*following on behind*] If only I'd thought of it before.

JUDY   Can't we ring up the station at the other end?

MR BROWN   We can. But knowing Paddington, he might get off anywhere.

MRS BIRD   Things just won't be the same without that bear.

MR BROWN   You can say that again!

[*He turns to leave, and as he does so,* PADDINGTON *pops up from behind the parcels and raises his hat.* MR BROWN *sees him and shines the torch in his direction*]

            Paddington!

PADDINGTON Hullo, Mr Brown.

THE BROWNS [*chorus*] Paddington!

JUDY   You didn't go after all!

PADDINGTON I did. But I missed the train. I seem to cause so much trouble that I thought you wouldn't want me to stay any more, so I thought I'd better go back to Darkest Peru.

[*He reaches behind the parcels and takes a jar of marmalade, which he puts in his suitcase. Then he holds up his picture of Aunt Lucy.*]

            I haven't even had time to pack properly.

MRS BROWN   Not want you to stay?

MRS BIRD   Of course, we want you to stay.

JUDY   Even Mr Curry wants you to stay. Don't you, Mr Curry?

MR CURRY   Well, er . . . Hmmmmmmmph.

MR BROWN   [*waving his torch in the direction of Paddington's photograph frame as he talks*]
            Besides, if you go, who's going to eat all the marmalade?

MRS BIRD   Exactly! The cupboard's full.

PADDINGTON   [*peering at the glass on the photograph excitedly*] Would you mind doing that again, Mr Brown?

MR BROWN   Do what again?

PADDINGTON   Wave your torch about.

MR BROWN   You mean . . . like that? [*He repeats the action*]

PADDINGTON   That's it! That's what I saw the other night! Oh, dear!

JUDY   Can anyone join in?

JONATHAN   Or is it a secret?

PADDINGTON   It's a reflection, Mr Brown. You see, when I shone that torch at my bedroom window the other night, I thought I saw someone signalling back at me. Only it wasn't . . . I thought it was the man who'd stolen your marrow. But it must have been the reflection from my own torch all the time . . .

MRS BROWN   [*looks at the others*] Paddington . . .

PADDINGTON   Yes, Mrs Brown?

MRS BROWN   You're incorrigible!

PADDINGTON   [*hotly*] I'm not, Mrs Brown. I'm a bear!

JUDY   And a jolly good bear at that. [*She takes his paw*]

JONATHAN   Hear! Hear! [*nudges Judy, takes Paddington's other paw, and together they lift him onto a box. Cue for song.* JONATHAN *and* JUDY *lead the others into* "For He's a Jolly Good Bear Cub" *as the play ends*]

CURTAIN

Songs

I Try So Hard

PADDINGTON I try so hard to get things right,
So why do things go wrong?
When I paint the ceiling, people stop and stare
Just because the whitewash gets into my hair.

AUDIENCE I try so hard to get things right,
So why do things go wrong?

PADDINGTON When I help the plumber, I feel such a fool,
What was once the kitchen, is now a swimming pool.

AUDIENCE I try so hard to get things right,
So why do things go wrong?

PADDINGTON When I do the cooking, why do people joke?
Just because the last lot all went up in smoke.

AUDIENCE I try so hard to get things right,
So why do things go wrong?

PADDINGTON People mock my gardening, when I'm planting seeds.
Pulling up the carrots, watering the weeds.

AUDIENCE I try so hard to get things right,
So why do things go wrong?

PADDINGTON Whenever there's a problem, I try to lend a paw,
But things always end up much worse than before.

ALL I try so hard to get things right,
So why do things go wrong?

Paddington Bear

He's here, he's there, he's Paddington Bear,
A rare sort of bear from Peru.
Paddington, Paddington, Paddington, there
Will never be another like you.

Cocoa in his thermos,
Sandwich in his hat,
Always pleased to greet you,
Likes to have an elevenses chat.
When you're next in London,
Look around and there
You will find a station
That has been named after this bear.

He's here, he's there, he's Paddington Bear,
A rare sort of bear from Peru.
Paddington, Paddington, Paddington, there
Will never be another like you.

Paddington's adventures
Drive our cares away,
He turns frowns to smiles and
Makes work seem a holiday.
He likes making toffee
For us all to share,
He sticks to his friends and
They stick to this marmalade bear.

He's here, he's there, he's Paddington Bear,
A rare sort of bear from Peru.
Paddington, Paddington, Paddington, there
Will never be another like you.

Paddington's adventures
Never seem to end,
Everybody loves him,
He's our very own favourite friend.
Life was very quiet till
He changed everything,
But we all enjoy it,
That is why we smile when we sing,

He's here, he's there, he's Paddington Bear,
A rare sort of bear from Peru.
Paddington, Paddington, Paddington, there
Will never be another like you.